Ready for a Picnic

Copyright © QED Publishing 2004

First published in the UK in 2004 by
QED Publishing
A division of Quarto Publishing plc
The Fitzpatrick Building
188–194 York Way, London N7 9QP

A Catalogue record for this book is available
from the British Library.

ISBN 1 84538 016 9

Written by Celia Warren
Designed by Alix Wood
Editor Hannah Ray
Illustrated by Elke Zinsmeister

Series Consultant Anne Faundez
Creative Director Louise Morley
Editorial Manager Jean Coppendale

Printed and bound in China

START
Reading

Ready for a Picnic

Celia Warren

QED Publishing

Grandma's Trip

Grandma packed her slippers,
her lipstick and her comb.
Grandma packed her toothbrush
and her bubble-bath foam.

Grandma packed her passport,
her bikini and some socks.
Grandma packed her camera
and her jewellery box.

4

Grandma packed her deckchair
and a picnic hamper,
then, last of all, before she left,
Grandma packed ... Grandpa!

5

I Like Eggs

Egg with sausages,
Egg with rice,
Egg with egg
If you like egg twice.

Egg with chips,
Egg on toast,
Egg on egg
If you like egg most.

6

Ready for a Picnic

One for a sandwich,
Two for a cake,
Three for an ice-cream by the lake.

Four for an apple,
Five for a pear,
Six for a picnic – see you there!

The Dizzy Hamster

"Tell me, little hamster, how does it feel
going round and round in your little wheel?"

"Well," said the hamster, "what I have found
is when the wheel stops then the room goes round."

Giraffe

I'd like my head to be up in the blue,
Giraffe, giraffe, I'd like to be you.

I'd like to be as tall as a tree,
Giraffe, giraffe, would you like to be me?

I like the way you pull funny faces,
Giraffe, giraffe, would you like to change places?

What Can I Be?

I can be a penguin and waddle as I walk,
I can be a parrot with a funny way to talk,
I can be a hamster and curl up small,
I can be a dog and bring you a ball,
I can be a monkey and swing from a tree
But, if you like, I can just be me.

Painting

I painted my daddy,
I painted my mummy,
but Mummy got cross
when I painted my tummy.

11

Off We Go

Up the hill

By the waterfall, then ...

Over the wall,

Roly-poly, Roly-poly,

Along the path,

All the way down.

12

Hats

Paper hats for parties,
Flowery hats for show,
Straw hats in summer,
Everywhere you go.

Hard hats for builders,
A white hat for a cook,
Woolly hats in winter,
Everywhere you look.

13

Riddles

The shape of a plate or a coin, the full moon or a bowl of soup, the shape of a button, the sun or a wheel, what shape is as round as a hoop?

A roof or the shape of the ear of a cat; three sides and three corners, what shape is that?

Landscape

My potato is an island.
The gravy is the sea.
The peas are people swimming.
The biggest one is me.

My carrots are whales
That make the sea wavy
But the big, brown blobs
Are LUMPS in the gravy!

Washing Up

Knives and forks and spoons in a jumble,
Dishes clatter, splash and tumble,
Bubbles in the bowl where fingers fumble,
Doing the washing up.
SPLASH!

Ten Bold Pirates

Ten bold pirates, all ship-shape,
Two got sea-sick
　　and that left eight.

Eight bold pirates up to their tricks,
Two met a shark
　　and that left six.

Six bold pirates tired of being poor,
Two found treasure
　　and that left four.

Four bold pirates feeling blue,
Two swam home again
　　and that left two.

Two bold pirates drinking rum,
They fell asleep
　　and that left none.

Garden Birds

Sparrow sings in the holly,
Starling sings in the oak.
Pigeon hops on the chimney pots,
Singing in the smoke.

Daffodil Dip

Dip, dip, daffodil,
Trumpet shout.
Dip, dip, daffodil,
You are OUT.

Dip, dip, daisy,
Petals all gone,
Dip, dip, daisy,
You are ON.

19

This Little Poem

This little poem you can keep in your hands,
Sometimes it wriggles and sometimes it stands.

It likes to wave, it loves to clap,
Then it falls asleep face down in your lap.

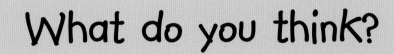

Can you remember all the things that Grandma packed?

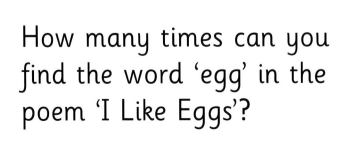

How many times can you find the word 'egg' in the poem 'I Like Eggs'?

What happened
to all the pirates?

Can you find any
words that rhyme
in the poem
'Ready for
a Picnic'?

Carers' and teachers' notes

- Encourage your child to help you to sort and categorize the poems by subject matter, e.g. animals, food, family.
- Together, think up pairs of rhyming nouns and use them to substitute items mentioned in the poem 'Grandma's Trip'.
- Collect a box of toys and use them as props for a 'Ready to Play' poem, using 'Ready for a Picnic' as a model.
- Together, search the poems for opposites, e.g. 'summer'/'winter'; 'up'/'down', etc.
- Use 'What Can I Be?' as the basis of a PE activity, adding further animal actions.
- Recite 'This Little Poem' with hand-actions. Substitute new actions, e.g. 'Sometimes it jumps …'
- Collect the hats mentioned in the poem on page 13 and encourage your child to help you to perform the poem, putting on the relevant hats as you read.
- Read 'Riddles'. Identify the shapes and find more circles and triangles in the illustration. Ask your child to draw a pattern of triangles, or to print with triangles cut from sponges, potatoes, etc.
- Write rhyming words from selected poems onto cards. Spread them, face up, on a table-top. Choose one card at a time and challenge your child to find the word's rhyming pair. Encourage your child to look at the ending of the words in order to work out whether or not they rhyme.
- Make an index of the poems' titles, making sure they are in alphabetical order.
- Ask your child to nominate his/her favourite poem from the book, and to learn it by heart. Choose a different poem and learn it, too. Use 'Daffodil Dip' to decide who will perform their poem first.
- Collect a list of prepositions, e.g. 'over', 'under', 'on', etc. Act as scribe to write a collaborative journey poem. Begin every line with a preposition, as in the first four lines of 'Off We Go'. Be adventurous – journey into space or under the sea.